THE LITTLE BOOK OF

JOY

First published in 2025 by OH
An Imprint of HEADLINE PUBLISHING GROUP LIMITED

1

Disclaimer:

Cataloguing in Publication Data is available from the British Library

ISBN 978-1-03542-266-1

Compiled and written by: Jason Ward
Editorial: Saneaah Muhammad
Designed and typeset in Dosis by: Stephen Cary
Project manager: Russell Porter
Production: Rachel Burgess
Printed and bound in China

Headline's policy is to use papers that are natural,
renewable and recyclable products and made from
wood grown in well-managed forests and other
controlled sources. The logging and manufacturing
processes are expected to conform to the
environmental regulations of the country of origin.

HEADLINE PUBLISHING GROUP LIMITED
An Hachette UK Company
Carmelite House, 50 Victoria Embankment, London EC4Y 0DZ

The authorised representative in the EEA is Hachette Ireland, 8 Castlecourt Centre,
Dublin 15, D15 XTP3, Ireland (email: info@hbgi.ie)

www.headline.co.uk   www.hachette.co.uk

THE LITTLE BOOK OF
JOY

FOR WHEN LIFE
WANTS TO CELEBRATE

CONTENTS

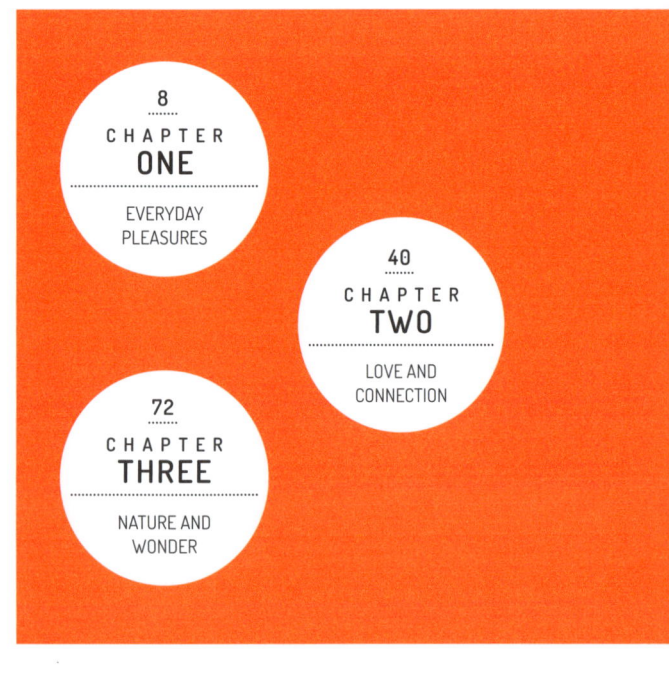

INTRODUCTION

Much of life is difficult. Sometimes those challenges are formative and help us become better versions of ourselves, and sometimes they just feel like the consequences of a world that is random, indifferent or cruel. It's just part of the contract, the trade-off we make, the price of the ticket.

But life isn't all uphill. From the everyday to the extraordinary – from our deepest passions to our toughest moments – there's always space for joy. It's like the air in our lungs: something simple and profound and available to everyone, regardless of their circumstances. It can be easy to take for granted or even ignore, but joy is *the* essential part of being alive. Joy, perhaps, could be best described as the love of being alive – the outright pleasure of being in your body, in this place, at this time.

The Little Book of Joy is a collection of thoughts on this idea: insight, beauty and humour gathered from centuries of thinkers. Hopefully something in these pages will inspire or move you, or give you comfort at a time when you need it; hopefully you will find something here that's *for you*.

CHAPTER

1

EVERYDAY PLEASURES

Because small joys are so, well, small, we overlook them. But they crowd into every part of the day, and our lives are enriched by paying attention to them.

How simple and frugal a thing is happiness: a glass of wine, a roast chestnut, a wretched little brazier, the sound of the sea. All that is required to feel that here and now is happiness is a simple, frugal heart.

Nikos Kazantzakis

We spend our life, it's ours, trying to bring together in the same instant a ray of sunshine and a free bench, in some oasis of public verdure.

Samuel Beckett

Happiness in this world, when it comes, comes incidentally. Make it the object of pursuit, and it leads us on a wild goose chase, and is never attained. Follow some other object, and very possibly we may find that we have caught happiness without dreaming of it.

Nathaniel Hawthorne

Oh! kangaroos, sequins,
chocolate sodas!

You really are beautiful! Pearls,
harmonicas, jujubes, aspirins!

Frank O'Hara

Dinnertime is the most
wonderful period of the day
and perhaps its goal –
the blossoming of the day.

Novalis

The discovery of a new dish does more for human happiness than the discovery of a new star.

Jean Anthelme Brillat-Savarin

We cannot be young twice; we cannot turn upon our steps, and go back to gather the garlands we gathered ten years ago. And, therefore, with a gaze over on the cross upon the distant hills, and a remembrance always of the shadow land that lies beyond, let us endeavour to be contented with small things, and to make ourselves happy in the pleasantness of simple pleasures.

Holme Lee

Things are such that someone lifting a cup, or watching the rain, petting a dog, or singing, just singing – could be doing as much for this universe as anyone.

Rumi

To be happy at home is the ultimate result of all ambition, the end to which every enterprise and labour tends, and of which every desire prompts the prosecution.

Samuel Johnson

Yes! in the poor man's garden grow,

Far more than herbs and flowers,

Kind thoughts, contentment,
peace of mind,

And joy for weary hours.

Mary Howitt

Young people now drink less, it's said, than for many generations. They're more sensible, it's said, more focused. I think, though, that they're just more fearful... One drink at lunch is rebellion. Two is sedition. Three is revolution. The boozy lunch may be rare now, but when a boozy lunch does come along, it's just *wonderful*.

Deborah Orr

Who can blame a man for eating too much red meat? You might just as well blame him for singing too loudly in the bath; it's part of what it is to be an exuberant human, living in fortunate times.

Zoe Williams

Avoid greatness; in a cottage there
may be more real happiness than
kings or their favourites enjoy.

Horace

Happiness was simply
something that occurred in a
well-regulated life.

Brian Aldiss

The bar is in full swing and floating rounds of cocktails permeate the garden outside until the air is alive with chatter and laughter and casual innuendo and introductions forgotten on the spot and enthusiastic meetings between women who never knew each other's names... Laughter is easier, minute by minute, spilled with prodigality, tipped out at a cheerful word.

F. Scott Fitzgerald

Forget not that the earth delights
to feel your bare feet and the winds
long to play with your hair.

Kahlil Gibran

Childhood itself is scarcely more lovely than a cheerful, kind, sunshiny old age.

Lydia Maria Child

Happiness is a good flow of life.

Zeno of Citium

Do not enjoy yourself. Enjoy dances and theatres and joy-rides and champagne and oysters; enjoy jazz and cocktails and night-clubs if you can enjoy nothing better; enjoy bigamy and burglary and any crime in the calendar, in preference to the other alternative; but never learn to enjoy yourself.

G. K. Chesterton

Surely everyone is aware of the divine pleasures which attend a wintry fireside; candles at four o'clock, warm hearth rugs, tea, a fair tea-maker, shutters closed, curtains flowing in ample draperies to the floor, whilst the wind and rain are raging audibly without.

Thomas De Quincy

I never get enough of the adrenaline rush of hearing good music played live and played loud like this. Hearing these songs again snatches me out of the day-to-day and helps me forget all the things I usually waste my time worrying about. As long as the music's playing I don't have to do anything except listen, relax, and enjoy myself.

David Moody

If you haven't learned to cook by the time you're thirty, you are insensible to the grace of living.

Christopher Fowler

The city is all right. To live in one

Is to be civilized, stay up and read

Or sing and dance all night and see sunrise

By waiting up instead of getting up.

Robert Frost

For my part, I travel not to go anywhere,
but to go. I travel for travel's sake.
The great affair is to move.

Robert Louis Stevenson

I cook with wine, sometimes
I even add it to the food.

W. C. Fields

The proper union of gin and vermouth is a great and sudden glory; it is one of the happiest marriages on earth and one of the shortest-lived. The fragile tie of ecstasy is broken in a few minutes, and thereafter there can be no remarriage.

Bernard De Voto

Take my hand. We will walk. We will only walk. We will enjoy our walk without thinking of arriving anywhere.

Thích Nhất Hạnh

Most people enjoy the inferiority
of their best friends.

Philip Stanhope

But what is happiness except the simple harmony between a man and the life he leads?

Albert Camus

I'm turning left. Look, everyone, my blinker is on, and I'm turning left. I am so happy to be alive, driving along, making a left turn. I'm serious. I am doing exactly what I want to be doing at this moment: existing on a Tuesday, going about my business, on my way somewhere, turning left.

Amy Krouse Rosenthal

CHAPTER
2

LOVE AND CONNECTION

Some people are said to light up a room when they enter; love can do the same thing to your whole life.

Oh, God, I know no joy as great as a moment of rushing into a new love, no ecstasy like that of a new love. I swim in the sky; I float; my body is full of flowers, flowers with fingers giving me acute, acute caresses, sparks, jewels, quivers of joy, dizziness, such dizziness.

Anaïs Nin

This inner progressiveness of love
between two human beings is a most
marvellous thing; it cannot be found by
looking for it or by passionately wishing
for it. It is a sort of Divine accident.

Hugh Walpole

Being with you and not being
with you is the only way I have
to measure time.

Jorge Luis Borges

I want to do with you what spring
does with the cherry trees.

Pablo Neruda

Oh god it's wonderful to get out
of bed and drink too much coffee
and smoke too many cigarettes
and love you so much.

Frank O'Hara

If you died it would be like my bones
had been removed. No one would know
why, but I would collapse.

Sarah Kane

Beauty crowds me till I die.

Beauty, mercy have on me!

Yet if I expire to-day

Let it be in sight of thee!

Emily Dickinson

We have a beautiful cosmos,
you and me.

Ivor Cutler

I answer one of your letters, then lie in bed in apparent calm, but my heart beats through my entire body and is conscious only of you. I belong to you; there is really no other way of expressing it, and that is not strong enough.

Franz Kafka

He must have smiled at me, though I don't really know, but I don't like to think that I would love someone who hadn't first smiled at me.

Jamaica Kincaid

People tend to stick to their own
size group because it's easier on the
neck. Unless they are romantically
involved, in which case the size
difference is sexy. It means: I am willing
to go the distance for you.

Miranda July

Elaine was too formidable... one
of the most intelligent, beautiful and
witty women I had ever met. I hoped
I would never see her again.

Richard Burton

Love is overflowing joy. Love is
when you have seen who you are.
Then there is nothing left except to
share your being with others.

Bhagwan Shree Rajneesh

You can have the best there is

But it's going to cost you all your love.

Bob Dylan

Nine-tenths of wisdom
is appreciation. Go find
somebody's hand and squeeze
it, while there's time.

Dale Dauten

Happiness does not await us all.
One needn't be a prophet to say that there
will be more grief and pain than serenity
and money. That is why we must hang
on to one another.

Anton Chekhov

Among those whom I like or admire, I can find no common denominator, but among those whom I love, I can: all of them make me laugh.

W. H. Auden

One's life has value so long
as one attributes value
to the life of others, by
means of love, friendship,
indignation and compassion.

Simone de Beauvoir

Of all the means which wisdom
acquires to ensure happiness
throughout the whole of life, by far
the most important is friendship.

Epicurus

Give me but a little cheerful company, let me only have the company of the people I love, let me only be where I like and with whom I like, and the devil may take the rest, say I.

Jane Austen

Stay close to those who sing, tell stories, enjoy life and whose eyes sparkle with happiness. Because happiness is contagious and will always manage to find a solution whereas logic can find only an explanation for the mistake made.

Paulo Coelho

Love is the axis and breath of my life. The art I produce is a byproduct, an excrescence of love, the song I sing, the joy which must explode, the overabundance – that is all!

Anaïs Nin

Let ev'ry man enjoy his whim;

What's he to me, or I to him?

Charles Churchill

The ineffable joy of forgiving and being forgiven forms an ecstasy that might well arouse the envy of the gods.

Elbert Hubbard

And you were a presence full of
light upon this earth

And I am a witness to your life
and to its worth.

John Darnielle

Gone, he kissed the air where
she had stood.

Ivor Cutler

The more we find to love,
the more we add to the measure
of our hearts.

Lloyd Alexander

When first we fall in love, we feel
that we know all there is to know about
life, and perhaps we are right.

Mignon McLaughlin

Love is not consolation, it is light.

Simone Weil

When I saw you I fell in love, and you
smiled because you knew.

Arrigo Boito

CHAPTER
3

NATURE AND WONDER

You don't need to trek into the wilderness to find nature – sometimes you just need to feel the breeze on your skin. The true miracle, surely, isn't the world we live in, but that we are lucky enough to bear witness to it.

I am glad you love the Blossoms so well. I hope you love Birds too. It is economical. It saves going to Heaven.

Emily Dickinson

No matter how sophisticated you may
be, a large granite mountain cannot
be denied – it speaks in silence to the
very core of your being.

Ansel Adams

If the stars should appear one night in a thousand years, how would men believe and adore, and preserve for many generations the remembrance of the city of God which had been shown! But every night come out these envoys of beauty, and light the universe with their admonishing smile.

Ralph Waldo Emerson

A sudden gust:
How big the world seems in a wind.

Kim Stanley Robinson

Nature is painting for us, day after day,
pictures of infinite beauty.

John Ruskin

The richness I achieve comes from nature, the source of my inspiration.

Claude Monet

There's joy in the mountains:

There's life in the fountains;

Small clouds are sailing,

Blue sky prevailing;

The rain is over and gone.

William Wordsworth

Leaf! you are so big! How can you change your colour, then just fall! As if there were no such thing as integrity!

Frank O'Hara

Isn't it enough to see that a garden is beautiful without having to believe that there are fairies at the bottom of it too?

Douglas Adams

Nothing in Nature is unbeautiful.

Alfred Tennyson

There is geometry in the humming of the strings. There is music in the spacings of the spheres.

Pythagoras

Those who contemplate the beauty of the earth find reserves of strength that will endure as long as life lasts. There is something infinitely healing in the repeated refrains of nature – the assurance that dawn comes after night, and spring after winter.

Rachel Carson

Never before have I lived through a storm like the one this night. The sea has a look of indescribable grandeur, especially when the sun falls on it. One feels as if one is dissolved and merged into Nature. Even more than usual, one feels the insignificance of the individual, and it makes one happy.

Albert Einstein

Things perfected by nature are
better than those finished by art.

Cicero

Sometimes, in a summer morning, having taken my accustomed bath, I sat in my sunny doorway from sunrise till noon, rapt in a reverie, amidst the pines and hickories and sumachs, in undisturbed solitude and stillness, while the birds sing around or flitted noiseless through the house, until by the sun falling in at my west window, or the noise of some traveller's wagon on the distant highway, I was reminded of the lapse of time. I grew in those seasons like corn in the night, and they were far better than any work of the hands would have been. They were not time subtracted from my life, but so much over and above my usual allowance.

Henry David Thoreau

The inaccessibility of this loch is part of its power. Silence belongs to it. If Jeeps find it out, or a funicular railways disfigures it, part of its meaning will be gone. The good of the greatest number is not here relevant. It is necessary to be sometimes exclusive, not on behalf of rank or wealth, but of those human qualities that can apprehend loneliness.

Nan Shepherd

The mountains are calling
and I must go.

John Muir

If you will stay close to nature, to its simplicity, to the small things hardly noticeable, those things can unexpectedly become great and immeasurable.

Rainer Maria Rilke

The world is full of poetry. The air is living with its spirit; and the waves dance to the music of its melodies, and sparkle in its brightness.

James Gates Percival

The universe is full of magical things patiently waiting for our wits to grow sharper.

Eden Phillpotts

I think it pisses God off if you walk by
the colour purple in a field somewhere
and don't notice it.

Alice Walker

People from a planet without flowers would think we must be mad with joy the whole time to have such things about us.

Iris Murdoch

Let's lie down on the bank of the river
and listen to water's pulse.

Linda Hogan

That is one good thing about
this world... there are always sure
to be more springs.

Lucy Maud Montgomery

Summer afternoon – summer afternoon; to me those have always been the two most beautiful words in the English language.

Henry James

Delicious autumn! My very soul
is wedded to it, and if I were a bird
I would fly about the earth
seeking the successive autumns.

George Eliot

Who ever breasted a snowstorm without being excited and exhilarated, as if this meteor had come charged with latent aurorae of the North, as doubtless it has? It is like being pelted with sparks from a battery. Behold the frost-work on the pane – the wild, fantastic limnings and etchings!

John Burroughs

CHAPTER
4

EMBRACING
LIFE

The advice to seize the day is always
vaguely terrifying, like you've somehow
been living wrong until now. The day
isn't there to be seized, it's there to be
lived in, with as much curiosity and
delight as you can muster.

You will do foolish things, but do them with enthusiasm.

Colette

Nature says thou shalt keep the air, skate, swim, walk, ride, run. When you have worn out your shoes, the strength of the sole leather has passed into the fibre of your body. I measure your health by the number of shoes and hats and clothes you have worn out. He is the richest man who pays the largest debt to his shoemaker.

Ralph Waldo Emerson

Within a little time must ye go by.

Stretch forth your open hands,
and while ye live

Take all the gifts that Death and
Life may give.

William Morris

The moment you wake up, right away, you can smile... You are aware that a new day is beginning, that life is offering you twenty-four brand new hours to live, and that that's the most precious of gifts.

Thích Nhất Hạnh

Whatever I do is done
out of sheer joy: I drop my
fruits like a ripe tree.

Henry Miller

I note, at the age of ten, a fully developed ability not quite to enjoy myself, a capacity I've retained intact ever since.

Alan Bennett

Live now, believe me, wait not till
tomorrow; Gather the roses of life today.

Pierre de Ronsard

Everyone runs around trying to find a place where they still serve breakfast because eating breakfast, even if it's 5 o'clock in the afternoon, is a sign that the day has just begun and good things can still happen. Having lunch is like throwing in the towel.

Jonathan Goldstein

The most difficult thing is the decision to act, the rest is merely tenacity. The fears are paper tigers. You can do anything you decide to do. You can act to change and control your life, and the procedure, the process is its own reward.

Amelia Earhart

Well, I can tell you about the river,
or we could just get in.

Bill Callahan

The secret for harvesting from existence the greatest fruitfulness and greatest enjoyment is – to live dangerously.

Friedrich Nietzsche

I was standing in front of the mirror. I dared myself to cut off my hair. I did it. Now I feel like I can do anything in the world.

Amy Krouse Rosenthal

The only reality is now, today.
What are you waiting for to be happy?
Happiness is not exuberant or noisy, like
pleasure or joy; it's silent, tranquil, and
gentle; it's a feeling of satisfaction
inside that begins with self-love.

Isabel Allende

I have many places where I sit and think, 'I have been here before, I am here now, and I will be here again.' These secret visits are a way for me to measure the wheel of the years and my passage through life. Sometimes on this voyage through life we need to sit on the deck and regard the waves.

Roger Ebert

Enjoy the present hour,
be thankful for the past,

And neither fear nor wish th'
approaches of the last.

Abraham Cowley

We cannot be happy if we expect to live all the time at the highest peak of intensity. Happiness is not a matter of intensity but of balance and order and rhythm and harmony.

Thomas Merton

On with the dance!
let joy be unconfined!

No sleep till morn, when youth
and pleasure meet,

To chase the glowing hours
with flying feet.

Lord Byron

It is good

To lengthen to the last a sunny mood.

James Russell Lowell

O for a life of Sensations
rather than of Thoughts!

John Keats

At Earth's great market where
Joy is trafficked in,

Buy while thy purse yet swells
with golden Youth.

Alan Seeger

After the horse dance was over, it
seemed that I was above the ground and
did not touch it when I walked.

Black Elk

I have drunken deep of joy,
And I will taste no other wine to-night.

Percy Bysshe Shelley

Running is many things to me: survival, calmness, euphoria, solitude. It is proof of my corporeal existence, my ability to control my movement through space if not time, and the obedience, however temporary, of my body to my will.

Audrey Niffenegger

I wanted movement and not
a calm course of existence. I
wanted excitement and danger
and the chance to sacrifice
myself for my love.

Leo Tolstoy

The only thing you know for sure is the present tense. That nowness becomes so vivid to me now, that in a perverse sort of way, I'm almost serene. I can celebrate life. Below my window, for example, at this season the blossom is out in full. It's a plum tree. It looks like apple blossom, but it's white. And looking at it, instead of saying, 'Oh, that's nice blossom,' last week, looking at it through the window when I'm writing, it is the whitest, frothiest, blossomest blossom that there ever could be. And I can see it. Things are both more trivial than they ever were, and more important than they ever were, and the difference between the trivial and the important doesn't seem to matter. But the nowness of everything is absolutely wondrous.

Dennis Potter

Life is either a daring
adventure or nothing.

Helen Keller

I'm in a wild mood tonight.
I want to go dance in the foam.
I hear the banshees calling.

Raymond Chandler

CHAPTER
5

FLOURISHING

To flourish is to *thrive*. This doesn't
just mean ticking off accomplishments,
but giving ourselves to our passions,
and the people around us.

Wonder is the beginning of wisdom.

Socrates

Love what you do and do what
you love. Don't listen to anyone else
who tells you not to do it.

Ray Bradbury

Only passions, great passions,
can elevate the soul to great things.

Denis Diderot

My dreams were all my own;
I accounted for them to nobody; they
were my refuge when annoyed –
my dearest pleasure when free.

Mary Shelley

Happiness is not achieved by
the conscious pursuit of happiness;
it is generally the by-product of
other activities.

Aldous Huxley

Set me a task in which I can put
something of my very self, and it is a
task no longer; it is joy; it is art.

Bliss Carman

The great end of all human industry, is the attainment of happiness. For this were arts invented, sciences cultivated, laws ordained, and societies modelled, by the most profound wisdom of patriots and legislators. Even the lonely savage, who lies exposed to the inclemency of the elements and the fury of wild beasts, forgets not, for a moment, this grand object, of his being.

David Hume

Hope elevates, and joy
Brightens his crest.

John Milton

Two things fill the mind with ever-increasing wonder and awe, the more often and the more intensely the mind of thought is drawn to them: the starry heavens above me and the moral law within me.

Immanuel Kant

In every life we have some trouble,
but when you worry you make it
double. Don't worry, be happy.

Bobby McFerrin

Money brings some happiness.
But after a certain point, it just
brings more money.

Neil Simon

Who is rich?
Those who are happy
with their portion.

Simeon ben Zoma

To be without some of the things you want is an indispensable part of happiness.

Bertrand Russell

It's an illusion to think that more comfort means more happiness. Happiness comes of the capacity to feel deeply, to enjoy simply, to think freely, to risk life, to be needed.

Storm Jameson

Joy is what happens to us when
we allow ourselves to recognize how
good things really are.

Marianne Williamson

The only way to find true happiness is to risk being completely cut open.

Chuck Palahniuk

Compulsion is not indeed the
final appeal to man, but joy is.
And joy is everywhere.

Rabindranath Tagore

There is one great truth on this planet: whoever you are, or whatever it is that you do, when you really want something, it's because that desire originated in the soul of the universe. The soul of the world is nourished by people's happiness.

Paulo Coelho

I sometimes try to be miserable
that I may do more work.

William Blake

The joy of life consists in the inevitable, continual triumph of new values.

Wassily Kandinsky

I, for one, live only by
and for happiness.

David Vogel

Accept your lot and make your mother happy! Run fast and make your god happy!

Sumerian proverb

Hope is itself a species of
happiness, and perhaps
the chief happiness which
this world affords.

Samuel Johnson

A change in the weather is
sufficient to recreate the world
and ourselves.

Marcel Proust

Taste the joy
That springs from labour.

Henry Wadsworth Longfellow

In a century or two, or in a millennium, people will live in a new way, a happier way. We won't be there to see it – but it's why we live, why we work. It's why we suffer. We're creating it. That's the purpose of our existence. The only happiness we can know is to work toward that goal.

Anton Chekhov

Tomorrow belongs to those of us who conceive of it as belonging to everyone; who lend the best of ourselves to it, and with joy.

Audre Lorde

We have it in our power to
begin the world anew.

Frank Cottrell-Boyce

CHAPTER
6

BEING HERE

So much of our days are taken up
by worries. This isn't irrational, but it
also isn't all there is. It's good to be
alive – honestly it is.

The butterfly counts not
months but moments, and
has time enough.

Rabindranath Tagore

Live in each season as it passes; breathe the air, drink the drink, taste the fruit, and resign yourself to the influences of each.

Henry David Thoreau

It's too nice of a night. Go outside and look around you. There's a 7/8ths full moon. It's cool and breezy and people are sharing cabs and touching each other innocuously just out of the sheer delight of being alive and having hands. There are people on the street right now earnestly debating what kind of matching group Halloween costumes they should wear because, and

I quote, 'the Halloween clock is ticking'. There are masquerades in our future. There are holidays to think about. It's too nice of a night to talk about anything that doesn't take place on a fire escape with a spider plant on it, in any voice other than a low tone while someone nearby smokes a cigarette.

Brie Williams

You are a miracle, and everything
you touch could be a miracle.

Thích Nhất Hạnh

Every day brings a chance for
you to draw in a breath, kick off
your shoes, and dance.

Oprah Winfrey

When you arise in the morning,
think of what a precious privilege
it is to be alive – to breathe, to think,
to enjoy, to love.

Marcus Aurelius

How strange it is to be anything at all.

Jeff Mangum

Life is not complex.
We are complex.
Life is simple, and
the simple thing
is the right thing.

Oscar Wilde

I love my past. I love my present.
I'm not ashamed of what I've
had, and I'm not sad because
I have it no longer.

Colette

Keep your heart in wonder at
the daily miracles of your life.

Kahlil Gibran

It is so great a thing to be an
infinitesimal part of this immeasurable
orchestra the music bursts the heart,
And from this tiny plosion all the
fragments join: Joy orders the disunity
until the song is one.

Madeleine L'Engle

The nicest thing about being
happy is that you think you'll
never be unhappy again.

Manuel Puig

The secret of happiness is to face the fact that the world is horrible, horrible, *horrible.*

Bertrand Russell

Life feels both sad and dark and
confusing and *more* than hopeful –
it feels like something totally incredible
could happen at any moment and
with no explanation.

Miranda July

When you have loved as she has loved,
you grow old beautifully.

W. Somerset Maugham

Yes, this planet is in a terrible mess.
But it has always been a mess.
There have never been any Good
Old Days, there have just been days.
And as I say to my grandchildren:
Don't look at me. I just got here.

Kurt Vonnegut

Life does not always meet our expectations, but that should not prevent us from seeking what happiness we can.

Richard Parks

Home is watching the moon rise over the open, sleeping land and having someone you can call to the window, so you can look together. Home is where you dance with others, and dancing is life.

Stephen King

What an interesting life I had.
And how I wish I had realized it sooner!

Colette

The platonic teenage party (platonic in the sense that it was the ideal party of which all others were mere imperfect copies) involved a rented room, a trestle table, a Dansette Bermuda or maybe even a proper discothèque (two Dansette Bermudas and a flashing light), some girls and a supply of Watney's Party Seven. It poured at random, got everywhere, and always ran out. But in its benign gleam, the music sounded better, the lights were softer, the girls more beautiful and potentially yielding, oneself manlier, one's friends friendlier, the night darker, the stars brighter, the moon fuller, the air warmer, the hour later, the future brighter, the present aching with that particular adolescent promise which does not need to be fulfilled to make it miraculous.

Michael Bywater

A man is a small thing
and the night is very large
and full of wonders.

Edward Plunkett

There are only two ways to live your life. One is as though nothing is a miracle. The other is as though everything is a miracle... I'm going with B.

Amy Krouse Rosenthal

God, what is all this talk put
out by the popes? Paradise is here,
my good man. God, give me
no other paradise!

Nikos Kazantzakis

I believe in beauty.
I believe in stones and water,
air and soil, people and their
future and their fate.

Ansel Adams

All deep things are song. It seems
somehow the very central essence of
us, song; as if all the rest were but
wrappages and hulls!

Thomas Carlyle

The aim of life is to live, and
to live means to be aware,
joyously, drunkenly, serenely,
divinely aware.

Henry Miller

Although the number of
unhappy days is endless, yet
life is better than death.

Sumerian proverb